Old DARVEL

by
Hugh Maxwell

This was the view when entering the 'Lang Toon' from the west around 1896. In the centre of the picture is the lace mill of Cleland, Campbell, and Co. Factories such as this used the powerloom which heralded the demise of the handloom weaving. At one stage there were over six hundred handlooms within the town and the 'clack' of the loom could be heard from all of the cottages both night and day. The old weavers had many customs such as meeting at certain street corners and also cooking enough porridge to last for at least a week. To do this they would pour it into the top drawers of a dresser, allowing it to set. Then each day they would be able to enjoy breakfast without having to cook. The porridge was never thrown away even if it was over a week old and was often mixed with treacle and whisky to make it palatable. *We are weavers all, and life is a loom/ Where the shuttle of years flies fast/ The yarn on the beam is the future's gloom/ The cloth on the roll is our past* – 'The Weaver', by local poet Tom Smith.

ACKNOWLEDGEMENTS

The author wishes to thank the staff of the reference department of the Dick Institute, Kilmarnock, and also the many people of Darvel who contributed information towards this book. The publishers wish to thank Stanley Zimmer for providing most of the pictures featured in this book.

SOME FURTHER READING

James Mair, *A Pictorial History of Darvel*, 1989.
John Woodburn, *A History of Darvel*, 1967.
Copies of the *Weekly Supplement and Advertiser for Galston* and also the *Irvine Valley News* held within the Dick Institute, Kilmarnock.

The stepping stones over the River Irvine gave access from the Morton Park (left) onto the Browns Road which is hidden by the trees on the right. The large concrete blocks were washed away during the heavy 'Lammas floods' which occurred in the early 1920s and which caused considerable damage to other neighbouring villages and towns on its course. The 'Broons Road' itself was constructed by the Browns of Lanfine and provided a very pleasant walk along the south bank of the river to Newmilns. The Brown family also built nearby Lanfine House and owned much of the land in this part of the Irvine Valley. They were generous benefactors to the local community and the construction of the 'Broons Road' provided work for many of the unemployed at a time of depression for handloom weaving.

INTRODUCTION

Darvel can trace the origins of its name back to around 1066. Following in the wake of William the Conqueror's invasion of England, the De Camlys family from the two communities of L'Odeon and D'Arville in Normandy travelled to Britain. Around a century later their descendants ventured north to Scotland. By this time the family's name had come to be known as Campbell and they settled in an area of Cuninghame they called Loudoun. They named the upper reaches of their land in the Irvine Valley as Darville, possibly because it reminded them of their ancestors' homeland in France.

Later, the main landowners of the area were the Loudoun Family of Loudoun Castle and in 1752 they granted twelve feus for the building of small cottages on the north side of the highway, either side of the position of the Cross in Darvel today. This was the beginning of the modern town and the initial occupants were families that were displaced from neighbouring 'ferm touns' because of the revolutionary land reforms being implemented by the landowners. Most quickly established themselves as handloom weavers and as more families were able to sustain a living from weaving linen cloth so more cottages were built. The hamlet quickly began to expand and an indication of this growth can be seen in the population numbers which increased dramatically from just a few inhabitants to four hundred by 1791 and then seven hundred by 1819.

Darvel became a Police Burgh in 1873 under the Lindsay Act and the General Police and Improvement Act. This allowed basic public order to be maintained as well as legislating improvements to streets, public wells, footpaths and the implementation of street lighting. The elected representatives were known simply as commissioners, although they became 'councillors' when the Town Council was created thirteen years later.

In 1870–73 a disastrous slump occurred within the handloom weaving industry due to a dramatic fall in the prices the weavers received for their finished goods. Out of Darvel's six hundred looms, only 226 survived and many residents experienced severe poverty and some emigrated or sought work in other towns and cities. Outbreaks of cholera and smallpox also struck the community at this time and many of the cottages were simply left abandoned while the streets became overgrown with grass and weeds. However, this period of unrelenting hardship and poverty was relieved by one of Darvel's own sons who dramatically transformed the weaving industry and in doing so brought great prosperity and success to the town and its inhabitants.

Born in 1844, Alexander Morton began working at the age of eight as a herdsman and farm labourer. He became a 'wabster' four years later and at fifteen used his own savings to buy a handloom. Within a few years he was distributing looms to other weavers and this enabled him to form links with the other 'wabsters' which would prove crucial to completing repeat orders for lace curtains, sometimes to the value of £4,000, which he would often obtain.

Morton frequently travelled to London to secure orders and on a visit in 1874 he was captivated by a demonstration of the 'Lever' powerloom lace machine. He quickly saw this as the future for the weaving industry and a machine was soon ordered and housed in premises at the Glen Brig. The company of Alexander Morton and Co. was formed and became so successful that despite quickly purchasing more machines, they could never meet the demand for their lace curtains. A new factory was later built behind Hastings Square and many of the handloom weavers soon found employment working the huge powerloom machines which could produce up to 120 pairs of lace curtains each week.

The success of this venture caught the imagination of other entrepreneurs and factories were built on sites throughout the whole town for machine production of lace and madras. Stirling Brothers, Alexander Jamieson and Co. and Cleland, Campbell and Co. were all formed before the end of the 1880s. A thousand people were soon employed in the textile trade and many natives returned with their families to find work and enjoy a higher standard of living than could be found elsewhere in the country. Twelve more factories were completed before 1915, although by this time there was such a shortage of housing within the town that a plea was made by the burgh council for the townspeople to convert all the old handloom workshops and any other small rooms to provide accommodation for the influx of people.

Prior to the outbreak of the Second World War, twenty factories were in operation, two manufacturing solely madras, three producing madras and lace, and fifteen manufacturing lace. These were the golden days of the industry with over 1,800 workers employed within the mills and associated trades such as cardcutting, designing and engineering. Half this number were young women. The population had also risen to 3,400 and the Irvine Valley as a whole was now producing 50% of all lace furnishings in Britain.

This prosperity did not last. In the years following the end of the war many of the factories were suddenly faced with much cheaper competition from overseas, changing fashions and the introduction of taxes in the form of tariffs. This resulted in over half of the mills closing down in the late 1960s and 1970s and the loss of all the associated trades. Those firms that still maintain the weaving tradition have been forced to diversify into the production of terylene, tartans, sports goods, blinds and yashmaks. There are at present six textile factories, only two of which still produce traditional lace.

It is not all gloom, however, because many of the sites left by the demolition of the factories have been transformed into residential housing schemes. This has brought a large number of families to the town and today Darvel is regarded as a pleasant place to live, surrounded by peaceful countryside. The population has also now stabilised at around 3,700.

A recent 'Old Darvel' exhibition held to mark the millennium attracted great interest from many local people and ex-residents and it is hoped that an old thatched handloom weaving cottage will be restored to create a permanent heritage centre for the town. This will enable future generations and visitors alike to remember and experience Darvel's remarkable history.

Main Street, Darvel, looking East.

On the left is the building of Thomas Fleming, a cheese and grain merchant who was also the agent for the Union Bank of Scotland which was also based there. Later, Mr Gray became the bank manager and, splendidly adorned in his black bowling hat with black suit and gloves, he was an instantly recognisable figure within the town. On the right is the corner of Temple Street, which is the only street within the town that gives a reminder of its ancient history: during the thirteenth and early fourteenth centuries the land that formed Darvel was in the possession of the Knights Templars until they were suppressed by Robert the Bruce in 1309. The east side of Temple Street was also where Alexander Morton built a large factory (replacing his premises at the Glen Brig) to exploit the expansion of the lace industry.

Main Street, Darvel (looking West)

The influx of people looking for work in the mills during the early years of the twentieth century meant that local shops and businesses thrived. A notice in a *Weekly Supplement and Advertiser for Galston* from July 1896 informed customers that 'William Smith (Tailor and Clothier) formerly of Burnbank Street, Darvel, has now moved to 57 and 59 West Main Street, Darvel. His new shop will enable him to show to advantage all the newest and latest styles of material for gentleman's wear. In stock are a splendid selection of Worsteds, Vicunas, Serges, Saxonys, Cheviots and the new 'Lovat' tweed. Also hats, caps, scarfs, collars, cuffs, fronts, umbrellas and braces. Parties bringing their own cloth will receive the same attention as if bought on the premises.' The building on the left housed one of the first shops of the Darvel Industrial Co-operative Society which was founded in 1840. As shown in the picture, the post office later took it over and it is now the premises of Walker and Connell, printers and stationers.

Hastings Square was the regular meeting place for members of the parish church cycling club every Saturday afternoon. On one occasion in 1905 an especially high turnout of about twenty-five members gathered on a mild October afternoon for the weekly run to Sorn. It was common for members to enjoy frequent stops en-route, often with tea being served by the ladies of the club. A little commotion was caused however when an accident occurred, not serious, to one of the ladies when going down a steep incline. The club spent some time at Mauchline before returning via Galston. Their first ever run, destination Larkhall, was on Saturday 29 April, 1900. The ladies probably rode the 'Thelma' ladies safety cycle while the men would have favoured the 'Mortone' gents cycle fitted with the patented parallel chain adjustment. In 1900 both of these models were advertised in the *Weekly Supplement and Advertiser* by Todd's ironmongers in Main Street.

The Cross, East Main St. Darvel.

At the turn of the twentieth century Darvel had many small grocers' shops such as Gemmell's, Wylie's, Dunning's, Morton's, Livingstone's and Rogerson's. It would have been unnecessary for the residents to shop outside of the town at that time. On the right of this picture of the Cross is one of the wells which was erected following the introduction of a gravitational water system in 1890. Iron pumps were placed at intervals of 100 yards alongside the main street next to the main supply pipe. These were used for many years before houses and shops were eventually connected. The wells were operated by a handle at the side which was turned. The protruding iron plate enabled pails to be filled without the bottom getting dirty from the pavement.

TOWNHEAD, DARVEL.

A gas supply was installed in the town in 1853. Pipes were laid in a deep furrow on either side of the pavements of the streets, but it was not until 1857 that street lighting was installed. The first lamplighter was Alex Martin who was paid £9 annually for this task, although he was also the town bell-ringer and town crier. In 1900 a notice was placed in the *Weekly Supplement and Advertiser*: 'Wanted – young man to learn the making of gas, wages 20/-, 22/-, and 24/-. Apply by letter to Andrew Cameron, Town Clerk.' Mr James Cochrane was the manager of the gas works, which stood on Ranoldcoup Road, at this time and out of a list of eighteen applicants James Lambie was selected for the job.

GLEN BRIDGE, DARVEL

This young boy is standing on the path of a popular local walk called 'roon the water's lip'. The tenements of Glen Terrace can be seen in the background and they still stand today. Just out of picture on the right stood the premises where Alexander Morton introduced his first powerloom into the town in 1875. It was bought for £1,050 from the manufacturers Sharman and Wilson of Nottingham and had to be transported by horse and cart from the nearest railhead at Newmilns. After many initial difficulties and problems the machine was launched into noisy, thunderous action in February, 1876. The factory was eventually demolished in the early 1990s and the Glenbrig private housing scheme now stands on the site.

The main road to Priestland, looking westwards back to Darvel. On the right of the picture is the Darvel corn mill which was powered by a small lade that ran alongside the road from Darvel Dam. David Neil was the last miller before the mill itself was badly damaged by fire in the 1920s and later demolished. Today, only a small wall marks the site of the lade and the mill. Private housing on George Young Drive and Green Bank Road has since been built in this area.

DARVEL MILL DAM.

The Mill Dam was located at the east end of the town between Darvel and the hamlet of Priestland. On the left the fence marks the location of the main road which is still in use today. The lade which ran from the dam along the northern side of the road to Darvel corn mill had to be frequently cleaned of silt and stones washed through by the river when it was in spate and in the summer young boys would often guddle there for brown trout.

FOOTBRIDGE OVER CHANGUE BURN, DARVEL.

Darvel was once a popular destination for many people seeking a quiet rural holiday. Travelling from Glasgow or further afield, people came to view the town's lace mills and also enjoy the peaceful countryside and riverside walks. This picture shows a footbridge in Changue Glen which is about a mile south-east of Darvel. Many of the town's workers went there to enjoy the fresh outdoor air away from the noise, dirt and long shift hours of the factories and the glen was a popular destination for young men camping at weekends.

PRIESTLAND, DARVEL.

In this picture of Priestland taken around 1904, the cottage and premises of Alan Smith the grocer at Roading Foot is on the right, while the second cottage on the left was a grocer's and sweetshop known as Gracie's, renowned locally for selling Boston Cream. The entrance to this shop and the other houses on this side of the street was via a small footbridge over a lade that was used to provide power for Priestland corn mill on the banks of the River Irvine. Little evidence remains of the mill today and the site is now occupied by a house. Priestland was initially only a small cluster of cottages occupied by people employed in agricultural work, but it has since grown into a desirable residential area with a population of over one hundred.

In this view of the town from around 1906 can be seen, from left to right, the steeples of the Easton Memorial and Darvel Central churches adjacent to the Main Street, built in 1885 and 1888 respectively. Next on the right smoke billows from the large chimney of Alexander Morton's factory, while in the centre are the chimneys of Morton Brothers, madras and tapestry manufacturers, and the gasworks. On the far right the chimney belongs to the bleachworks which were built by James Cleland on the banks of the River Irvine in 1904. The large factory that can be seen in the foreground, right of centre, is Cleland, Campbell and Co., madras and lace manufacturers.

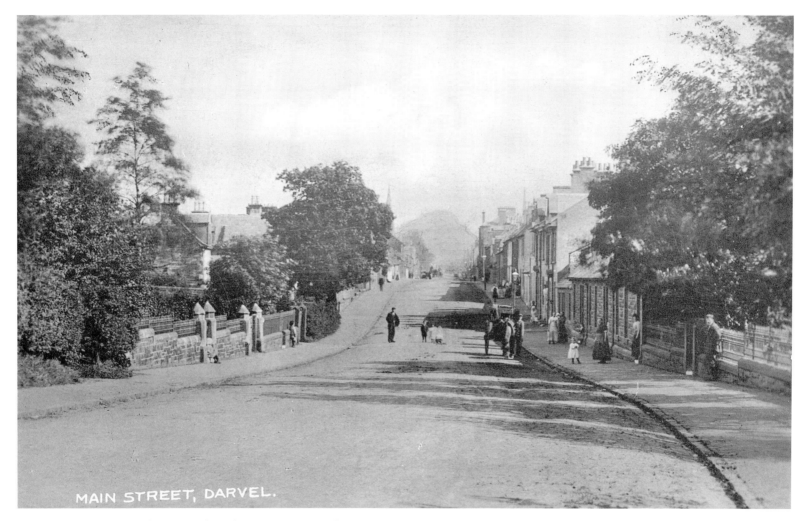

MAIN STREET, DARVEL.

'Toonfit' around 1910, looking east along the main street. At this time Darvel could lay claim to the idea of becoming a health resort. There surely must have been something special in the local air and water as the combined ages of the twelve eldest inhabitants in 1900 amounted to 1,058 years, an average of just over 88 years which was remarkable for that time. The oldest inhabitant was ninety-four! Much of the original housing seen in this picture still stands, the only change to this part of town being the appearance of the Dublin council housing scheme which was built after the Second World War.

The sandstone cottages of Burn Road, built around 1900. While these are unchanged, they are surrounded on all sides today by the modern private houses of Gilliland Road, Woodburn Court, Anderson Drive and Braes Court Avenue, and Campbell Street now links Burn Road with Jamieson Road. However, on the left the Matthew Burn still flows down into the town as it has done for many centuries past.

Burnbank Street, Darvel

Burnbank Street was built around 1890 as the town began to expand, branching out from the main street. The street is so named because the houses on the left side near the top were built on the edges of the Matthew Burn. Almost all of the old tenements on the right have been replaced with modern housing and McLauchlan Court has also since been built on this side of the street. At the top of the street can be seen Wilson's the butchers and the Turf Hotel on West Main Street. The hotel had the distinction of being the first building in Darvel to be roofed with 'Tulloch flags' or slates.

Alex. Jamieson & Co. Ltd. Darvel, Ayrshire.

C572

Alexander Jamieson and Co. was established in 1887. They were makers of fine madras curtains and also weaved tapestries in the form of curtains, tablecovers and antimacassars. The business was initially established in Glasgow before transferring to Darvel. Between sixty and seventy people were employed at the factory's powerlooms, although there was an equal number of handloom weavers producing lace under contract to the company within their own workshops (it wasn't long before the factories squeezed out demand for handloom lace and this kind of weaving ceased altogether). The factory soon grew to become the largest factory in Darvel, employing about 350 workers to produce lace and madras. It is still in operation, although under different ownership. The small building in the bottom right corner is the old fire station located on Burn Road. It was established by the burgh council to protect the many thatched roofs of the town. The railway station with its turntable, goods shed, sidings and ticket office can also be seen in the centre of the picture.

In the background of this view of West Donington Street can be seen on the right the offices and factory buildings of Alexander Jamieson and Co., with its large brickwork chimney prominent above the houses. Further up are red sandstone tenements which are still unchanged today, followed, in the foreground, by the Original Secession Church and manse which was built in 1883. Just out of picture is the old public school; the young boy is standing at the gates to the playground. Alexander Fleming went to school here in the 1890s and while there he was involved in a collision with a boy, sustaining a broken nose which altered his appearance permanently. Fleming was born at Lochfield Farm near the town in 1881. In 1928 he made his tremendous discovery of penicillin, the wonder drug which revolutionised medicine and has saved millions of lives. In 1946 he became the first ever Freeman of the Burgh of Darvel and a memorial garden was sited in Hastings Square to commemorate his magnificent achievement.

East Donington Street. As a burgh Darvel enjoyed much prosperity and growth in the early 1900s. The population had risen steadily to over 3,000 from a figure of only 2,000 in 1890. Sixteen factories were in full production and many workers were employed in long shifts, six days per week to fulfil increasingly large orders. Madras, tapestry, chenille, and lace were being manufactured into table covers, piece goods, antimacassars, and window and portiere curtains in both white and neutral tints. *The commerce o' Darvel is kent far an' wide,/ The Nottingham lace, an' the gauzy sheniel,/ Has procured me a fame, an' respect for my name,/ That only the future will fully reveal.* – 'Darvel's Lament' by Thomas Love.

DARVEL PUBLIC SCHOOL

Darvel Public School was erected by the Loudoun School Board and was officially opened on 5 January, 1904, to cater for the much increased educational needs of the town. It was declared open at eleven o'clock and after the opening ceremony a short programme of songs, recitations and physical drill was performed by the scholars. One of the songs sung was 'Ye banks and braes'. The school occupies a very attractive and commanding position at the corner of Jamieson Road. The building itself cost around £10,000 and was built from Ballochmyle red sandstone. Originally on the ground floor there were large cloakrooms, lavatories, and six classrooms for 350 scholars with a similar arrangement on the second floor. The boys entered by the west door, the girls by the east. It functioned as a junior secondary school for children between the ages of five and thirteen. The building is still in use today as a primary school and has changed very little in appearance.

This photograph from around 1920 looks east along the Main Street. On the right can be seen the Buttercup Dairies, Jack Robertson's Newsagent and adjacent to that Lawson's fish shop and then Gibson and Reid's, French cleaners and dyers. The cart outside may have been a delivery vehicle belonging to one of these businesses. On the opposite side of the street the trees and railings hide the E.U. Congregational Church (built 1889) and on its left is Tom Paterson's fruit shop. On the near left is the picture house which was extremely popular with large queues of people often waiting outside on the street. The *Weekly Supplement and Advertiser* always carried an advert detailing the latest films and their screenings at the cinema. In July 1923, for example, *The Sporting Duchess* which starred Alice Joyce was well received. It was a racing picture and attracted a large crowd on its Saturday screening. Wednesday's house was also full for *The Goddess of the Lost Lake* and *The Lamplighter.*

Lammie Brothers, the outfitters at the corner of West Main Street and Temple Street. David Lammie can be seen standing in the doorway to his shop. Locals came to know when a sale was on when they would hear children in the streets shouting, 'Lammie's trousers down again – come and see his bargains'. Other drapers in the town included A. Smith and Son, Wm. Davidson, and James Mair of West Main Street. They found a steady market in the many young men and woman who were employed within the mills and who wanted to spend their hard earned money on the latest and best of fashions for the regular dances held in Darvel and the neighbouring towns.

On Friday 30 June, 1905, William Morton performed the opening ceremony of the town hall. The occasion was celebrated by a procession of local children, led by the burgh band, to the public park for an afternoon of sports. In the evening a soiree, concert and ball was held at the hall with Miss Mary Finlay, the famous Scottish soprano, providing the entertainment. The building was erected under the auspices of the Darvel Art and Science Society with the intention of handing it over to the town council for use by the community. Robert Mair and Sons were the contractors and a Mr T.H. Smith of London was the architect. The total cost was £15,000. Today the hall houses the local library and council office, and is still very much at the heart of community activities.

MAIN STREET. DARVEL.

Main Street looking towards the Cross with Hastings Square on the right, *c.*1906. Where the men are standing in the centre of the picture, near the junction of Ranoldcoup Road, was where Richard Tarbet had his fruit and sweetie shop. Many of the town's natives aged eighty or more still remember Mr Tarbert's son, Peter, who was confined to his bed through poor health. A mirror was strategically placed within his room enabling him to lie there and look out onto the bustling street below. Once word spread of this people would often walk and ride past, waving and shouting up at his window in the knowledge that he would be lying there watching them.

WEST MAIN STREET AND MEMORIAL, DARVEL.

92832, J.V.

In the 1920s a war memorial was erected in Hastings Square in front of the parish church and opposite the town hall. It is an obelisk of Aberdeen granite standing thirty feet high. The panels of bronze bear the names of the 112 men who fell in the Great War. The unveiling ceremony was performed by General Sir Aylmer Hunter-Weston in front of the thousands of people who had assembled en masse from all the Irvine Valley towns. The memorial was later inscribed with the thirty-one names of those who perished during the Second World War. It still stands there today but is now flanked on the right by the Alexander Fleming memorial garden and on the left by the Dagon Stone, a large upended chunk of stone that has a round stone attached to the top with an iron dowel. Some say it is merely a huge boulder while others attach superstitious beliefs and powers to it.

In this 1920s view looking west along Main Street the pavements are busy but the road is fairly quiet with no congestion. However, accidents were by then starting to become a daily occurrence. In September 1920 the *Weekly Supplement and Advertiser* reported that, while going on his rounds with the breadvan, John Croly, an employee of the Darvel Industrial Co-operative Society, collided with a motor car belonging to John Mair, a motor hirer of Newmilns, and being driven by his daughter Kate. Happily, neither drivers were seriously injured although Croly was thrown from his van and the front of Mair's car was smashed and one of its wheels was buckled!

Hastings Place at the foot of Ranoldcoup Road, *c*.1908. On the right are the railings of Mair's Free School which was established in 1868 by trustees for Alexander 'Merchant' Mair to provide education for the children of Darvel. Alexander Mair created his fortune from trading direct, probably in locally produced handloom products, with the West Indies where he also supplied local shopkeepers with sugar beet, fruit, coffee and tobacco. The school is still in use for nursery education. On the left is the wall preceding the entrance to the old gasworks which opened in 1853. The towering gasworks chimney was a prominent feature within the town and the works provided power for street lighting and supplies from it were later installed within most houses and shops. The works are long gone and the site is now occupied by the bowling club and premises of the regional water authority.

The sawmill on the River Irvine dated back to the beginning of the nineteenth century and was in continual operation until the Second World War. It was located at the foot of Ranoldcoup Road just before the old sandstone bridge. A small lade enabled waterpower to be used to operate the large circular sawblade within the mill. Johnnie Rankin was the last sawmiller and he was mostly engaged in cutting trees from the nearby Lanfine Estate. The site has now become Bankview Crescent, a small private housing scheme.

DARVEL BURGH BAND: SCOTLAND'S PREMIER COMBINATION, 1922.

On a Saturday in April 1922 the Darvel Burgh Band, with their celebrated conductor Herbert Bennett, attended the Glasgow Charities Association's contest at Glasgow cattle market. Sixteen of Scotland's premier bands were in attendance. The test piece was 'Memories of Britain'. Darvel were drawn to play ninth and on finishing their piece they were given loud applause from the large audience. The band was awarded first prize for outstanding merit and the decision was received with tremendous cheering. A handsome silver shield, valued at £150, was awarded. The following June the band attended the finals for the world championship at the Kelvin Hall in Glasgow. Thirteen of Britain's best bands were competing and the test piece was Wagner's 'The Valkyrie'. The Burgh Band won third prize, giving them precedence over all the other Scottish bands and this caused a great stir. On returning home a large crowd gave a very enthusiastic reception as this was the first year that any Scottish band had won a place in the final three.

PUBLIC PARK AND RANOLDCOUP ROAD, DARVEL.   A.7276.

The Morton Park was gifted to the town in 1892 by Alexander Morton and Co. It was well planned with surfaced paths and gardens, children's paddling pool, sandpit, swings, chute and a large shelter to protect people from the rain. It also had its own drinking fountain and ample benches for seating. In this picture, taken from the Browns Road can be seen the steps leading down to the large 'Rab's Pool'. This was very popular with the boys for swimming during the summer while the girls' pool, known as 'Lassucks', was located further upstream.

MAIN STREET, DARVEL.

92833. J.V.

Main Street looking west around 1918. On the left can be seen the distinctive Darvel Co-operative Society delivery van used by the bakers. It would be loaded with fresh morning baking before doing the rounds of the various streets, factories and outlying farms and cottages. At this time the salesman would have been Jimmy Valance. On the right can be seen the sign for the once popular Young Men's Christian Association, although this building was later demolished and replaced with more modern housing.

Kirkland Road, looking North, Darvel

The bottom of Kirkland Road at its junction with East Main Street, *c.*1920. These red sandstone tenements were built to provide housing for the many families who chose to live in the town at this time and are still unchanged today. The small boy standing on the Main Street shows that the roads were still relatively quiet and uncongested. Children would often play 'chuckie stanes' which involved collecting five smooth, rounded white quartz pebbles from the nearby river, throwing them up into the air and trying to catch them all before they struck the ground. A Darvel version of a local jingle frequently sung by children around Halloween was 'Haleen, Haleen, this nicht at e'en, three wee witches on the green, yin black, yin green, and yin playin' the tamborine'.

In this photograph taken around 1910 Kirkland Road seems an idyllic, peaceful quiet street branching out into the countryside. This tranquillity was soon shattered on Saturdays when large crowds came to see Darvel Juniors play on the Kirkland Road pitch. They are undoubtedly the oldest surviving junior football club in Ayrshire, being formed in the season 1889–90 through the amalgamation of the Glen Thistle and Royal Albert football teams. In 1893–4 and 1894–5 the team won the Ayrshire Cup Trophy. It produced many excellent players, most notably Alex and Nicol Smith who would both join Rangers and also play for Scotland. This tradition was further strengthened when Sammy Cox also later signed for Rangers and played for Scotland. Kirkland Road became a quite countryside street again when Recreation Park was opened in 1919 in another part of town. Darvel Juniors still play at this park today.

Damage by Flood at Darvel Dam, August, 1920.

Not since 1895 had there been such a big spate on the River Irvine as occurred on 17 August, 1920. Considerable damage was done and the dam at Priestland was broken up and carried off. Some of the local factories also suffered damage. From early morning until evening the rain continued and conditions changed for the worse overnight. The unemployed were given work by the Town Council to repair the damage caused by the floods.

LOUDOUN HILL AND VIADUCT.

The viaduct below Loudoun Hill carried the line of the Caledonian Railway Company and connected Darvel to Strathaven. It stood for many years as a landmark until it was considered unsafe and demolished with considerable difficulty in 1986. Loudoun Hill is a conspicuous conical mound, an old volcanic plug, with a turbulent past. In 1307 an encounter took place there between the 1,200 strong army of Robert the Bruce and 3,000 English troops under the command of the Earl of Pembroke. Bruce was victorious and the confrontation became known as the Battle of Loudoun Hill. The car is parked on what is still the present main road.

DARVEL FROM N.W.

After the First World War Darvel's lace industry began to expand again with firms such as Smith and Archibald, McInnes Textiles and Smith and Cleland building factories within the town. In this photograph which dates from around 1930 the old quoiting ground by the railway embankment can be seen in the foreground. It was laid out on the old clay pit and up until the 1950s was very popular with the annual tournament on the third Saturday in August bringing competitors from far afield. Darvel won the Scottish Cup on many occasions with champion players such as Andrew Connell, who on one occasion was suspended for playing solely in competitions instead of for the club. Such was his accuracy, Andrew could be relied on to win by as much as eighteen to twenty-two shots. Playing in a team with his brother William, they were virtually unbeatable! The quoiting ground was later to become the site of Lochore Terrace.

A.4625.

TURF HOTEL & WEST MAIN STREET, DARVEL.

The Turf Hotel was originally built in 1781 as a house for Robert Wilson before alterations to its frontage around 1850 resulted in its appearance today. Before the opening of the railway station a twice-a-day brake service with extra runs on a Saturday connected Darvel with the station at Newmilns. The brake would stop at the Turf Hotel. In the early 1900s Mr John Murray took over the lease of the Turf Hotel stables and continued to operate a hiring and posting establishment as before. Later, as cars became popular, a petrol pump was placed outside on the street with a small lane giving access to the hotel car park and garage which were formerly used for stabling horses. The hotel also operated a taxi service. It has had many changes of ownership over the years but is still very popular with both locals and travellers.

BURN ROAD, DARVEL.

A view of Burn Road taken from the railway banking, c.1905. In the background can be seen 'The Braes', home of Alexander Jamieson. In 1923 Jamieson retired after thirty-three years on the burgh council, thirty of which were as provost. Many of the owners of the factories built large houses in and around the town, for example Lintknowe owned by William Morton and Gowanbank which was occupied by Alexander Morton. Also built were The Grange (for James Cleland of Cleland, Campbell & Co.), Kirkland Park and Fernilea. Today these magnificent houses still stand as evidence of the prosperity that the town once enjoyed.

DARVEL PUBLIC SCHOOL.

92839. J.V.

Up the hill just behind the school was Pond Braes, the site of the old curling ponds. Members played regularly for the Peesweep Medal which had been donated by the older Glen Water Club and often enthusiasm was so high amongst the competitors that arrangements were made to have their dinner brought up to the ponds. Many games were carried on late into the darkness of night when a clear moonlit sky would illuminate the ice for the players. Sadly the game became less fashionable and the club was closed in the early 1900s due to lack of numbers and interest.

MAIN STREET, DARVEL.

A.4622.

The main street in the 1940s, brimming with activity as a double-decker bus from Kilmarnock passes through, distinctive in the two-tone maroon livery of the Western S.M.T. Co. Ltd.   Passengers enjoyed frequent services although bus drivers had to regularly negotiate streets full of cyclists, carts and pedestrians as well as other motor vehicles. In the early 1950s an appeal by the burgh council, published in the *Weekly Supplement and Advertiser*, was made to all bus users to prevent accidents. They were told to wait in the queue, wait until the bus stopped at a proper bus stop before getting on, never to get on or off at traffic lights, wait until other passengers got off, help the young ones and the elderly, behave quietly and sensibly in the bus and to refrain from riding on the platform.

DARVEL FROM THE EAST, WITH JOHN MORTON CRESCENT   B 3166

John Morton Crescent was built in the years between 1928 and 1934, the first of the large council schemes built within the town and totally financed by the burgh council. After the slump of the late twenties and early thirties the lace industry was once again beginning to thrive. Modern housing was needed as the population had increased dramatically from about 1,400 in 1850 to nearly 3,000 by the end of 1940. Another large scheme was built at the top of Kirkland Road and was named Glen Crescent after the Glen Water which flows nearby. Paterson Terrace and Hutchison Drive were also completed. Today there have been only superficial changes to the area in the upgrading of the houses to meet today's living standards.

Darvel and Public Park.

Alexander Morton had initially established his lace factory in the east end of the town but because of the popularity and demand for lace he purchased land behind Hastings Square to build this new factory. It was the largest in the county and employed over eight hundred workers as well as several expert specialists. The lace produced was far superior to that made elsewhere and the products sold well throughout the world. Alexander Morton and Co. had control over a very large market both at home and abroad with commercial establishments at 74 Buchanan Street, Glasgow, 89 Newgate Street, London, and 874 Broadway, New York. Each building had a large office and warehouse to effectively display the company's vast range of products.

Engine no. 40579 with a train for Ardrossan at Darvel Railway Station in August, 1959. June 1896 saw the completion of the railway from Newmilns to Darvel. The contractors, Messrs Boyd and Forrest, carried out the work under the supervision of Mr Melville, the engineer of the Glasgow and South Western Railway Company. It took two and a half years to complete and was about two miles in extent with seven bridges between the starting point at Newmilns and the terminus at the head of Jamieson Road. A cake and wine banquet was held in the station house by the directors at the official opening and a celebratory gala day was also held in the town. Trains were referred to as 'down trains' or 'up trains', depending on their direction on the line. The line was extended to Strathaven in May 1905. The train in the picture became known locally as the 'Ardeer Special' because it took workers down the valley to Nobel's dynamite works at Ardeer. The line was closed in 1964.

Townfoot, *c.1950*. An incident during the night of Monday 13 August, 1956, shocked the town's residents. 'Two killed when American plane crashes on moor south-east of Darvel' was the *Irvine Valley News's* headline. The aircraft was a twin-engined Douglas Invader being flown from Iceland to France to join the French Air Force. Edgar Flanagan was the American pilot, accompanied by a Canadian navigator, W.A. Taylor. Constable Hunter of Darvel police station was alerted along with Mr Logan, factor of Lanfine Estate. The wreckage was eventually spotted in a dip between the hills south of Distinkhorn, about 4 miles from Darvel. The body of one man had been burned beyond recognition while the other man was found under a wing. Due to the difficulty of the terrain the bodies had to be removed by helicopter. Even today the wreckage can still be seen, partly buried in the deep peat.

WEST MAIN STREET, DARVEL

D 1936

This view shows West Main Street looking east towards Loudoun Hill. On the left can be seen Miller's the bakers while across the junction of Burn Road is Reid's Newsagents, Wilson's the butchers and then the Turf Hotel with its pavement petrol pump. On the right side of the street a man can be seen looking into Lex Barclay's Jewellers shop, while further on some young mothers stand at the corner of Burnbank Street and West Main Street, perhaps just returned from a pleasant walk around the Morton Park.

CHILDRENS' CORNER, MORTON PARK, DARVEL.   A.7277.

This photograph was taken from Ranoldcoup Road. On many occasions a travelling circus such as Pinder's International Circus would have a one-day stand in the children's park just off the Morton Park. The Big Top with its sawdust ring delighted both young and old. Many Sunday schools also used the park for day trips during the summer, travelling from as far as Glasgow and Clydebank. A small deposit was required to be given to the burgh council and provided the park was left tidy and in good order at the end of the visit this was returned.

WEST MAIN STREET AND TOWN HALL, DARVEL.

B.3155.

By the time of this picture, taken around 1960, Darvel still had twenty lace and madras factories in operation. It was a time of great change with household fashions dictating a demand for more modern artificial materials such as terylene rather than lace. As in the past many of the factories invested greatly and adopted these changes, installing new machines and training workers. This ensured the continued survival of an industry dating back to the time of the handloom weaver. On the right can be seen William Gebe's, plumbers and ironmongers, while next door is Pettigrew's the delicatessen and grocers. On the left at the corner of Hastings Square can be seen Walker and Connell's, the printers and stationers which is still going strong today.